# The PDA Space

"Our mission is that you feel supported and validated.
We are here to walk the path with you and
guide you to the support you need."

**Nicola Reekie, Founder of The PDA Space**

**(www.thepdaspace.com)**

## Autistic Realms

"Advocating for a better understanding of neurodivergence and mental health in education for young people and families.

Creating spaces for people to feel connected and accepted where differences are embraced.

Promoting neurodiversity affirming, identity-first language to support good mental health."

# Helen Edgar
# (www.autisticrealms.com)

# CONTENTS

4     Introduction

5     Importance of Neurodiversity Affirming Language

6     Identity First Language

7     What is Neurodiversity?

10   What is Neurodivergence?

13   Glossary

22   Abbreviations

25   Importance of Connections

26   References & Signposting

27   The PDA Space Summit Speakers 2023

30   Acknowledgements

# INTRODUCTION

I am Helen, and I developed Autistic Realms as a platform to advocate for a better understanding of neurodivergence and mental health in education. I am working to promote the importance of a neurodiversity-affirming culture in schools to support teachers, children/young people, and their families. I previously worked as a primary teacher for twenty years (in SEN settings) and am a parent of two neurodivergent children.

Nicola and her team have set up the fantastic PDA Space Summit 2023. The PDA Space Summit is a wonderful demonstration that shows what can be achieved when so many amazing people and different minds come together to support each other. The PDA Space provides a support network for families and professionals to develop a deeper understanding of Autism and PDA.

Please see the website for further details about The PDA Portal and other exciting news and resources. (www.thepdaspace.com)

## Disclaimer

*Autistic Realms reflects my experiences and personal interpretations of the knowledge and resources I have found valuable as a parent and teacher. I am not a medical professional or therapist. Please seek professional specialist advice if you have concerns or need further support and information.*

# Importance of Neurodiversity-Affirming Language

It can be challenging as a parent/carer when you discover that your children are different and struggling more than others. They may have been diagnosed as being Autistic, ADHD, PDA profile, Dyslexic, having Sensory Processing Differences, something different, or any combination of these; you may still be exploring and trying to identify their needs and may be realising some similarities within yourself and exploring your own identity.

Being a parent can feel overwhelming and confusing. It is like entering a new world. You may be reaching out for support online by typing in keywords such as 'Autism or PDA' but then discovering a new language and vocabulary you have not encountered before.

As professionals, using language and terminology can also take time to keep current. It is essential to reflect neurodiversity-affirming language in your practice and when writing reports to families whilst considering and respecting individual preferences and how people personally identify. There can be anxiety about using the 'wrong' vocabulary; hopefully, this guide will help.

Neurodiversity-affirming language supports good mental health. It may be a different way of using language and describing people than you have previously used or read about. I have listed some great neurodiversity-affirming websites at the end of this glossary.

# IDENTITY FIRST LANGUAGE

## Autistic Realms
### Language Matters

Person WITH Autism
=
Person First Language

Person ON the Autistic Spectrum
=
Person First Language

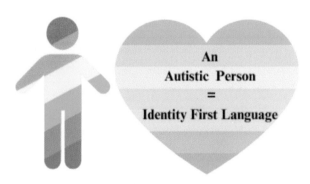

An
**Autistic Person**
=
**Identity First Language**

Identity first language is often preferred in the
Autistic community.
Using affirmative language supports
good mental health.
However, it is always important to respect a person's
preferred way of identifying.

# WHAT IS NEURODIVERSITY?

The term **neurodiversity** was coined by sociologist Judy Singer in her work, *NeuroDiversity: The Birth of an Idea* (1998).

The terms **neurodivergent** and **neurodivergence** were coined in 2000 by Kassiane Asasumasu, a neurodiversity activist.

The **rainbow infinity symbol** is often associated with a celebration of neurodiversity. Many neurodivergent people use it as an affirming symbol of acceptance and pride.

# Neurodiversity Includes Everyone

**Neurodiversity:** refers to the diversity of minds in the whole human population. It is a scientific fact that everyone is different and thinks differently to each other.

*"Neurodiversity is the diversity of human minds, the infinite variation in neurocognitive functioning within our species."*

**Neurodiverse:** As a society, we are neurodiverse; everyone is different.

*"A neurodiverse group is a group in which multiple neurocognitive styles are represented."*

**Neurodivergent:** Individuals may be described as being neurodivergent.

*"Neurodivergent, sometimes abbreviated as ND, means having a mind that functions in ways which diverge significantly from the dominant societal standards of "normal.""*

**Neurodivergence:** the state of being neurodivergent (i.e. Autistic, ADHD, OCD).

All quotes from Nick Walker, ***Neuroqueer Heresies*** (2021).

# WHAT IS NEURODIVERGENCE?

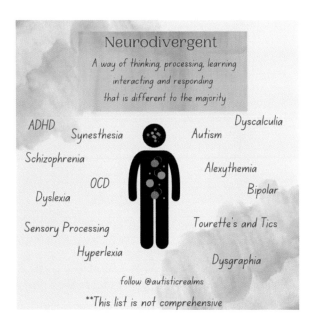

**Neurodivergence** is an umbrella term that covers all the different ways the body and mind interpret and respond to the world. This includes (but is not limited to); Autism, ADHD, Dyslexia, Dyspraxia, and OCD.

If you are **neurodivergent,** you will have a different way of thinking, processing, and responding to the world than others who are not neurodivergent. For example, if you are autistic, you will think, process and respond differently to non-autistic people.

# Neurodiversity Affirming Language is Inclusive

# Language Matters

| instead of... | think... |
|---|---|
| person with autism | → autistic person |
| high / low functioning | → specific needs |
| intervention | → support |
| co-morbidity | → co-occuring |

autisticrealms@gmail.com

# GLOSSARY

**Ableism:** discrimination experienced by people who are disabled.

**Attention Deficit Hyperactivity Disorder (ADHD):** a difference in neurology affecting attention, thinking, processing, and impulse. (Many don't see this as a disorder; instead, they see it as having differences).

**Alexithymia:** difficulties identifying, understanding, and expressing your emotions or/and those of others.

**Aphantasia:** an inability or difficulty to visualise mental images.

**Apraxia:** difficulties with motor planning (e,g., gross motor movements to walk/sit and apraxia of speech).

**Autism** is a difference in neurology that means you experience and respond to the world differently than non-autistic people. Differences include social interaction, communication and sensory processing, and ways of thinking (*monotropism*). Autistic needs are fluid and will change depending on the impact of the environment and other people.

**Autistic Inertia:** difficulties starting, stopping, or changing activities. You may feel 'stuck' in a channel of thought or activity (*see monotropism*).

**Autistic Overload** (may be called a meltdown): an external response to stress /sensory/social/ communication overload which may result in a person being unable to communicate, engage in activities, or complete executive functioning tasks;

senses may be heightened or lowered and behaviour responses affected.

**Burnout:** a period of intense sensory, social, emotional, and physical overwhelm that results in exhaustion and difficulties with *executive functioning,* memory, attention, and a change of capacity to communicate and regulate sensory input. It is brought on by periods of unmet needs. Burnout can lead to anxiety, depression, and other mental health difficulties. It takes time to rest, regulate and recover or heal.

**Double Empathy Problem:** a concept developed by Damian Milton (2012) that explains the differences in communication and socialisation between autistic and non-autistic people. Rather than the previous assumption that autistic people have no empathy and lack social skills, this concept explains that it is the difference between autistic and non-autistic people's way of communicating and socialising that can cause misunderstandings.

The emphasis should not be on autistic people to change their communication to be understood by non-autistic people. Instead, everyone needs to develop a deeper understanding of each other and be more inclusive.

**Dyscalculia**: difficulties related to understanding numbers and difficulties with maths.

**Dysgraphia**: difficulties with writing skills, and letter formation, can affect spelling and word choice (other fine motor skills may be efficient).

**Dyslexia**: a specific learning disability that means you have significant difficulties with reading, writing, and spelling.

**Dyspraxia:** difficulties with balance and coordination. It can also affect the planning and processing of motor tasks.

**Echolalia**: repetition of echoing words/sounds back to someone or self.

**Ehlers-Danlos Syndrome (EDS)** is a group of inherited conditions affecting the joints and connective tissues.

**Executive functioning:** a cognitive process that determines the ease and ability of planning, prioritising, focusing, organising, and carrying out tasks to meet a goal (e.g., washing, dressing, cooking, organising, and carrying out work).

**Hyperlexia:** a deep fascination with letters and words, accompanied by reading far earlier than peers. Reading skills may far exceed comprehension skills.

**Hypermobility Spectrum Disorder (HSD)**: a group of conditions related to joint hypermobility (JH).

**Hypersensitivity:** a more intense / heightened response to sensory stimuli, to the point it could feel very uncomfortable or even painful (e.g., light/sound/taste/touch/smell/movement/pain).

**Hyposensitivity:** a lower response to sensory stimuli, may be unaware of pain or not as responsive as you may expect (e.g., light/sound/taste/touch/smell/movement/pain).

**Identity first language (as opposed to person-first language):** this means putting a person's identity first. For example, to use identity-first language, you would use the term 'Autistic person', not 'person *with* autism' (which is person first language).

Identity first language is often considered preferable in the Autistic community, but it is always good to ask someone how they prefer to identify and respect their choice.

**Info-dumping**: a term often used to describe an autistic person sharing their deep knowledge and enthusiasm for their particular interests, often involving communicating on a single topic for long periods.

**Interoception:** relates to a person's ability to understand and interpret internal body signals and sensations. If you have difficulties with interoceptive awareness, you may not understand your body signals to know if you are hungry, thirsty, hot, cold, need the toilet, or are in pain.

**Intersectionality:** how multiple identities interact and affect a person and their relation to other people and the world around them (e.g., race, gender, age, nationality, and many other differences).

**Low demand:** a flexible approach (parenting or professional) where you intentionally decrease demands and provide a low arousal environment to reduce stress and anxiety. A low-demand approach is about meeting the needs of the person, not conforming to the expectations of others at the expense of mental health.

**Masking:** the act of consciously or unconsciously suppressing authentic autistic identity and needs in an attempt to fit into the social norms of other people. Masking is detrimental to mental health over a long period.

**Misophonia**: a hypersensitivity to sound stimuli (e.g., hearing someone eating may feel painful).

**Monotropism:** an affirming theory of autism (developed by (Murray, Lesser & Lawson, 2005) which could be seen as the core element of the autistic experience. The theory highlights that autistic people naturally have monotropic minds (a single attention channel). This allows a deep hyper-focus on areas of particular interest and enables autistic people to enter a 'flow state', which can help regulate the mind and body. It also explains some aspects of *autistic inertia,* such as difficulties changing channels of attention (the ability to refocus on tasks or other thoughts).

**Neurodiverse:** a group of people who think and respond differently to the world. Society is neurodiverse.

**Neurodiversity:** refers to the diversity of minds in the whole human population. It is a scientific fact that everyone is different and thinks differently to each other. As a society, we are neurodiverse.

**Neurodivergent:** having a mind that processes, thinks, and responds to the world in a different way (diverges) from the majority of the group /population.

**Neurodiversity Paradigm:** is a perspective that understands, accepts, and embraces the differences of everyone. Within this theory, it is believed there is no single 'right' or 'normal' neurotype, just as there is no single 'right' or normal gender or race. It rejects the medical model of seeing differences as deficits. It also recognises the same dynamics and inequalities that occur in society. Social, cultural, racial, and gender inequalities are also seen in those that are neurodivergent (see Nick Walker's work, *Neuroqueer Heresies*, 2021, for further info).

**Neurodiversity Movement:** social justice movement driving forward the ethos of the neurodiversity paradigm working for equality and inclusion for everyone.

**Neuromajority:** (sometimes referred to as **neurotypical**, although the idea of there being a 'typical' mind is sometimes debated): often used to describe people that are not neurodivergent, i.e. the majority of the population.

**Neurodiversity affirming**: promoting and valuing the ideas behind the neurodiversity paradigm and embracing inclusivity.

**Obsessive Compulsive Disorder** (OCD): a neurodivergence where a person experiences intrusive obsessive thoughts that trigger compulsions to try and relieve the anxiety caused.

**Pervasive Drive for Autonomy (PDA)** / sometimes referred to as **Pathological Demand Avoidance** (although this has negative connotations in the language used): PDA is widely understood to be a profile of autism, where people also "need control which is often anxiety related. This means they may be driven to avoid everyday demands and expectations, including things they want to do or enjoy to an extreme extent. People tend to use approaches that are 'social in nature' to avoid demands." *(This is an adapted definition from www.pdasociety.org.uk)*

**Proprioception**: is the body's ability to sense and understand its location, movements, and actions in relation to the space around them.

**Rejection Sensitive Dysphoria (RSD)**: refers to an intense emotional response related to actual or perceived rejection and heightened sensitivity to criticism/ any negative reaction.

**Scripting:** this can be a form of *masking* to try and fit into a social group. However, rehearsing, practising, and preparing what to say before a social situation can also help reduce anxiety.

**Sensory avoidance**: intentionally withdrawing from sensory experiences that don't make the person feel good or gives them discomfort/pain.

**Sensory diet**: an occupational therapist may create a 'sensory diet', an individual programme of ideas and activities to help regulate a person's sensory system depending on their needs.

**Sensory / Social overload:** (sometimes referred to as a *meltdown or shutdown*): a response to experiencing more social/sensory input that a person can manage. If an autistic person is experiencing a sensory /social overload, they will need time to rest, regulate and recover in a way that is right for them.

**Sensory processing**: an individual's interpreting and responding to various sensory signals and stimuli.

**Sensory seeking**: intentionally searching out sensory experiences that help make a person feel good.

**Sensory sensitivity**: depending on the individual's response to sensory stimuli at the time, some senses may be heightened and make the person feel discomfort or pain. This could cause some people to avoid certain situations and stimuli (e.g., sounds may be louder / certain textures may feel painful, etc.).

**Situational mutism:** a person's inability to produce speech in specific contexts.

**Shutdown**: an internal response to stress /sensory/social/ communication overload which may result in a person being unable to communicate, engage in activities, or complete executive function tasks; senses may be heightened or lowered.

**Special interest** (sometimes referred to as a **hyper-focus** or **passion**): an all-consuming hyper-focus for an autistic person that can bring great joy within a monotropic flow state (single channel of thought), a natural state for an autistic mind). Engaging in special interests provides opportunities for autistic people to regulate and gain deep knowledge or skills in a particular activity/topic. It can be an excellent opportunity to socialise and communicate with others that may share the same interest.

**Stimming:** refers to repetitive sensory-seeking behaviours that help to regulate the mind and body.

**Synaesthesia:** describes the mixing or overlapping of the senses (e.g., sound to colour). It is complex, and there are many forms of synaesthesia.

**Time processing difficulties:** often associated with ADHD, where a person has difficulty processing and understanding the passing of time.

**Tics**: repetitive muscle movements that result in sudden body jolts or vocalisations.

**Tourette's Syndrome**: a syndrome that causes a person to make involuntary sounds and movements called tics.

**Transition:** a change from one activity to the next or from one environment to another.

**Trauma-Informed:** Trauma-informed practice is an approach to health, care, and educational support based on the understanding that trauma exposure can impact an individual's neurological, biological, social, and psychological development.

*This glossary is not comprehensive but has hopefully provided you with an overview of some of the key vocabulary you may encounter in The PDA Space Summit 2023, hosted by The PDA Space.*

# ABBREVIATIONS

**AAC**: Alternative Augmentative Communication

**ACE**: Adverse Child Experiences

**ALN:** Additional Learning Needs

**ALNCo**: Additional Learning Needs Co-Ordinator (Wales)

**ASC / ASD**: Autism Spectrum Condition/Disorder

**ASN**: Additional Support Needs

**ADHD**: Attention Deficit Hyperactivity Disorder

**CAMHS**: Child Adolescent Mental Health Service

**EBSA:** Emotional-Based School Avoidance

**Ed Psych**: Educational Psychologist

**EOTAS**: Education Other Than At School

**EHCP**: Education Health Care Plan

**FSW:** Family Support Worker

**HLTA:** Higher Level Teaching Assistant

**IDP:** Individual Development Plan (Wales)

**IEP**: Individual Education Plan (also PEP, different schools may use other terms for this)

**LA:** Local Authority

**LGBTQIA+:** lesbian, gay, bisexual, transgender, queer or questioning, intersex, or asexual. The '+' holds space & recognition for other diverse gender and sexual identities and relationship styles.

**MLD:** Moderate Learning Difficulties

**OT:** Occupational Therapist

**PCP:** Person-Centred Planning

**PEP:** Personal Education Plan (also IEP, a different school may use other terms for this)

**PMLD:** Profound and Multiple Learning Disabilities

**PRU:** Pupil Referral Unit

**SLT / SALT:** Speech and Language Therapist

**SEMH:** Social, Emotional, Mental Health

**SEN:** Special Educational Needs

**SENCo:** Special Educational Needs Co-ordinator

**SEND:** Special Educational Needs and Disabilities

**SLCN:** Speech Language Communication Needs

**SLD:** Severe Learning Difficulties

**SpLD:** Specific Learning Difficulty

**TA:** Teaching Assistant (sometimes referred to as **LSA** Learning Support Assistant or **LSP** Learning Support Practitioner)

This list of abbreviations is not comprehensive but has hopefully provided you with an overview of key vocabulary you may come across during The PDA Space Summit 2023.

Written from lived experience as a parent and teacher through the knowledge and research shared within the neurodivergent community. I am not a medical professional or therapist. Always seek professional advice if you have any concerns or need further support.

## IMPORTANCE OF CONNECTIONS

# *Remember...*

It is important to remember that our relationships and connections with others are at the heart of everything.

Regardless of any labels, diagnosis, or vocabulary, the quality of the relationships and connections we create with people is essential and can make a positive difference.

Everyone is different; no label or diagnosis can capture a person's spirit. Moving away from pathological language and embracing neurodiversity-affirming language is essential to support good mental health.

*"Connection is the energy that exists between people*
*when they feel seen, heard, and valued; when they can*
*give and receive without judgment; and when they derive*
*sustenance and strength from the relationship."*
*Brene Brown*
*Rising Strong, (2015)*

# REFERENCES & SIGNPOSTING

www.aucademy.co.uk

www.autism.org.uk

www.autisticparentsuk.org

www.amase.org.uk

www.bdadyslexia.org.uk

www.ehlers-danlos.org

www.padlet.com/spectrumgaming/epic-autism-resources

www.familypathway.co.uk

www.kelly-mahler.com

www.neuroqueer.com

www.ocdaction.org.uk

www.pdasociety.org.uk

www.sedsconnective.org

www.spectrumgaming.net

www.stimpunks.org

www.thrivingautistic.org

www.youngminds.org.uk

# THE PDA SPACE SUMMIT SPEAKERS 2023

**Amanda Hind** - Navigating life as a Black mixed-heritage, a late-diagnosed autistic woman

**Asher Jenner** -PDA and inclusion...Why has it been vital to me?

**Catrina Lowry** - The Other 29

**Christina Keeble** -No, I don't need to be more consistent!

**Corrina Wood** - PDA, intolerance of uncertainty and CUES©

**David Gray Hammond & Tanya Adkin** - Autism, PDA, and addiction

**Debs Bamford** - Safeguarding with a twist .

**Dr Theresa Kidd -** PDAers Reaching Adulthood: Contributing Elements for a Successful Transition

**Hannah Harris -**Why Collaboration = Yes

**Helen Edgar & Viv Dawes -** Autistic Burnout - Supporting Children and young people

**Julia Caro -** Inclusion: Puzzles and contradictions

**Julia Daunt** - Making Sense of Sensory Processing Difficulties (SPD)

**Kate Denny** - The Warm Model

**Kay Aldred** - Working with the nervous system to understand and support regulation

**Kyra Chambers** -Collaborative approaches in mental health care

**Laura Hellfeld & Scott Neilson** - When Demands Make Eating Hard

**Libby Hill -** Using Poly-vagal theory to explain PDA and selective mutism

**Lindsay Guttridge -** How can parents deal with feeling excluded?

**Dr Naomi Fisher & Heidi Steel** - 4 things that your children need for their learning to SOAR

**Nicola Reekie** -Feeling excluded as a PDA parent

**Paula Rice** - True inclusivity doesn't fit in a predefined box

**Rachel Gavin & Cathie Long** - Fabricated or Induced Illness - Practice Guide

**Riko Ryuki** - The difference between PDA & ADA and why it matters

**Roanna Brewer** - The PDAers guide to navigating the education

**Sally Cat & No Pressure PDA** - PDA and trauma

**Sally-PDA talk** - When I Want To Be Included

**Suzan Issa** - PDA and the nervous system

**Tigger Pritchard** - True inclusion in education, peers and staff

**Tori Rist** - How to create an inclusive school

**Tracey Chadwick** - Doing EBSA differently

**Kristy Forbes** - Tuning into neuro-affirming family culture for PDA

*booklet published before the event. Speakers may be subject to last-minute changes as needed.*

# ACKNOWLEDGEMENTS

*Thank you to everyone for attending The PDA Space Summit 2023.*
*Thank you to our wonderful team of speakers*
*for sharing their knowledge and experience.*
*Together we can create a more understanding and inclusive future.*

I would like to thank all the fantastic people that I have met through the online neurodivergent and autistic community, especially Nicola Reekie, who is the founder of The PDA Space and organised the amazing The PDA Space Summit 2023. (www.thepdaspace.com).

I'd also like to thank Elsa Torres (www.familypathyway.co.uk ) & David Gray-Hammond (www.emergentdivergence.com) for reviewing this guide.

Also, thanks always to my wonderful family for their continued support of my work with Autistic Realms. *(www.autisticrealms.com)*

*"The PDA Space mission is that you feel supported nd validated. We are here to walk the path with you and guide you to the support you need".*

Nicola Reekie, Founder of The PDA Space

Written by Helen Edgar

Published for The PDA Space Summit May 2023

www.autisticrealms.com

© 2023

Printed in Great Britain
by Amazon